Pebble®

Out in Space

The Stars

by Martha E. H. Rustad

Consulting Editor: Gail Saunders-Smith, PhD

Consultant: Roger D. Launius, PhD
Senior Curator, Division of Space History
National Air and Space Museum
Smithsonian Institution, Washington, D.C.

Capstone
press®

Mankato, Minnesota

Pebble Books are published by Capstone Press,
151 Good Counsel Drive, P.O. Box 669, Mankato, Minnesota 56002.
www.capstonepress.com

1 2 3 4 5 6 13 12 11 10 09 08

Library of Congress Cataloging-in-Publication Data
Rustad, Martha E. H. (Martha Elizabeth Hillman), 1975–
    The stars / by Martha E.H. Rustad — Rev. and updated.
    p. cm. (Pebble books. Out in Space)
    Summary: "Simple text and photographs introduce stars and their features" —
Provided by publisher.
    Includes bibliographical references and index.
    ISBN-13: 978-1-4296-1720-8 (hardcover)
    ISBN-10: 1-4296-1720-9 (hardcover)
    ISBN-13: 978-1-4296-2816-7 (softcover)
    ISBN-10: 1-4296-2816-2 (softcover)
    1. Stars — Juvenile literature. I. Title.
QB801.7.R87 2009
523.8 — dc22   2007051320

Note to Parents and Teachers

The Out in Space set provides the most up-to-date solar system
information to support national science standards. This book
describes and illustrates stars. The photographs support early
readers in understanding the text. This book also introduces early
readers to subject-specific vocabulary words, which are defined
in the Glossary section. Early readers may need assistance to read
some words and to use the Table of Contents, Glossary, Read More,
Internet Sites, and Index sections of the book.

Table of Contents

4

Twinkling Lights

Stars twinkle in
the night sky.
They look like
tiny dots of light.

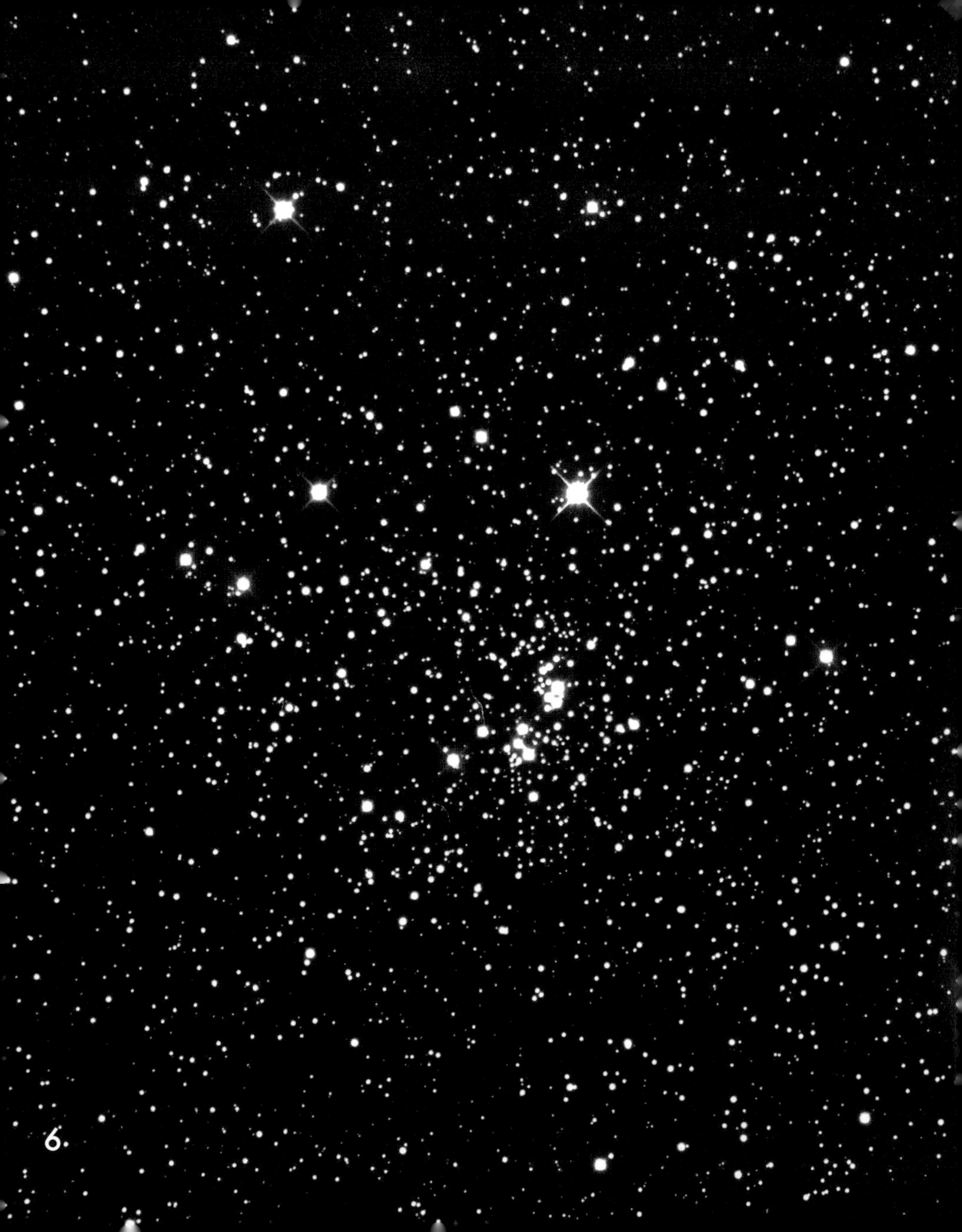
6

Space is full of stars.

Some stars are bright.

Some stars are dim.

8

What Is a Star?

A star is a huge ball
of gases in space.
The gases burn.
They give off light
and heat.

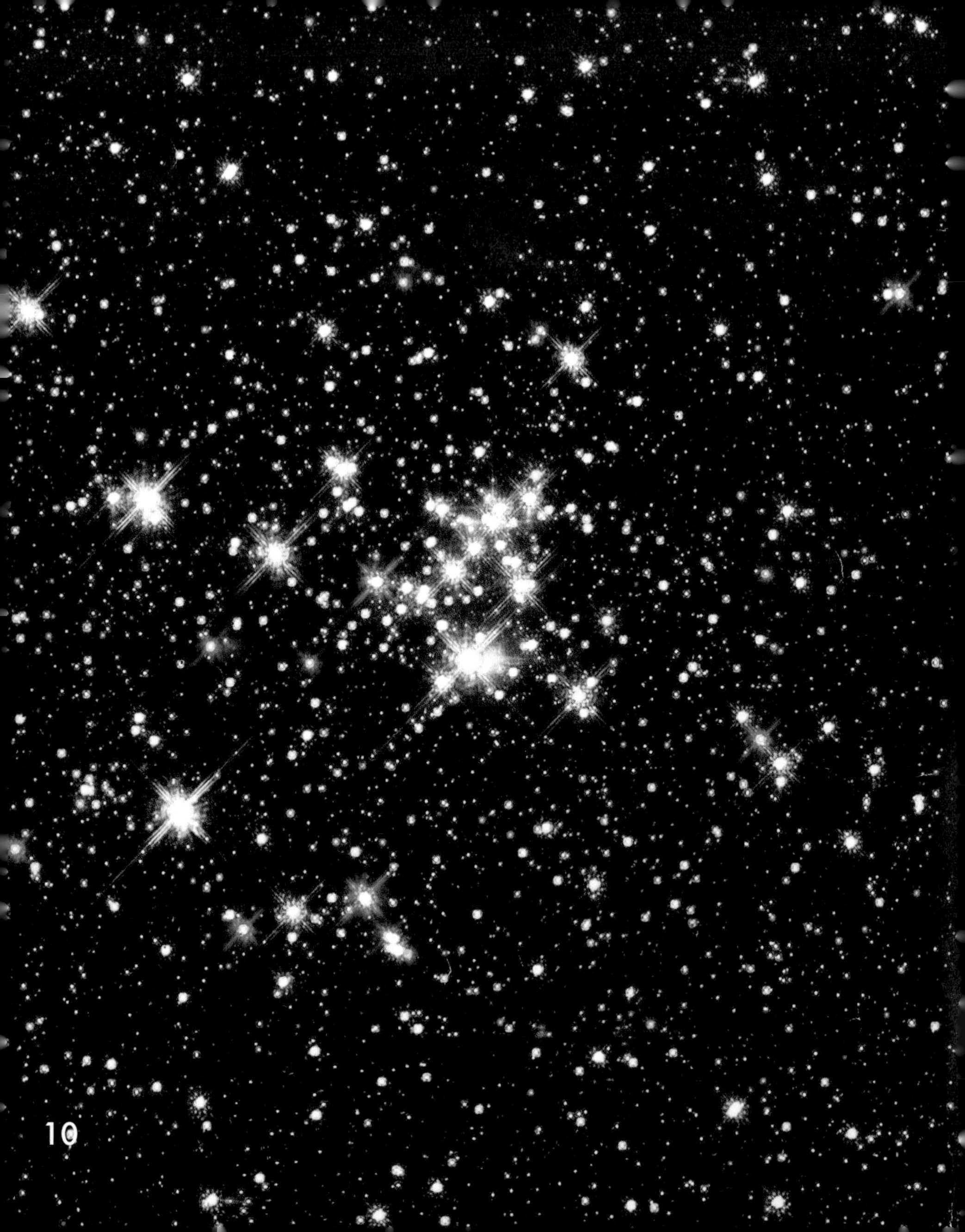

Stars are white, blue,
red, yellow, or brown.
Blue stars are the warmest.
Red stars are the coolest.

The Sun is a yellow star.
It is the closest star
to Earth.

The Life of Stars

Stars begin as dust
and gases in space.
Clouds of dust and gas
come together
to make stars.

16

Some stars
group together
in clusters.

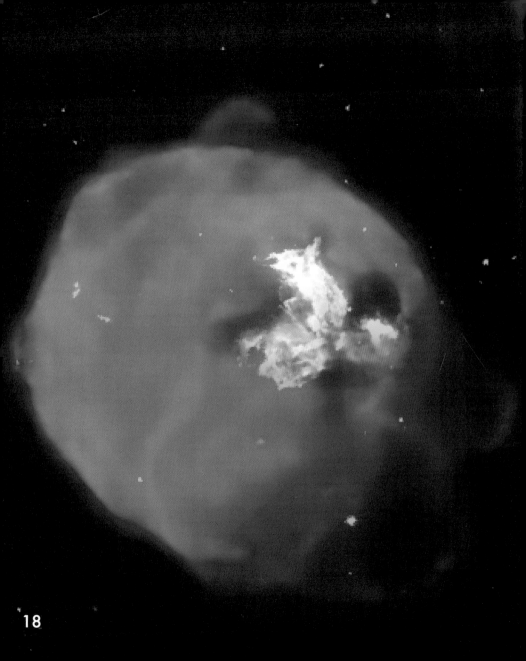

Stars grow larger
as they grow older.
Some stars blow up
when they die.

Most stars live for billions of years.

Glossary

cluster — a group of stars that are close together; a star cluster may contain 100 stars or more than 1 million stars.

dim — somewhat dark; dim stars are not very bright.

Earth — the planet we live on

gas — a substance that spreads to fill any space that holds it

twinkle — to shine or sparkle; stars look like they twinkle because of movement in Earth's atmosphere.

yellow star — a medium-sized star; the Sun is a yellow star; the temperature of the Sun is about 10,500 degrees Fahrenheit (5,800 degrees Celsius).

Read More

Adamson, Thomas K. *Stars.* Exploring the Galaxy. Mankato, Minn.: Capstone Press, 2007.

Bredeson, Carmen. *What Are Stars?* I Like Space! Berkeley Heights, N.J.: Enslow, 2008.

Rau, Dana Meachen. *Spots of Light: A Book about Stars.* Amazing Science. Minneapolis: Picture Window Books, 2006.

Internet Sites

FactHound offers a safe, fun way to find Internet sites related to this book. All of the sites on FactHound have been researched by our staff.

Here's how:

1. Visit *www.facthound.com*

2. Choose your grade level.

3. Type in this book ID **1429617209** for age-appropriate sites. You may also browse subjects by clicking on letters, or by clicking on pictures and words.

4. Click on the **Fetch It** button.

FactHound will fetch the best sites for you!

Index

Word Count: 121
Grade: 1
Early-Intervention Level: 14

Editorial Credits
Katy Kudela, revised edition editor; Kim Brown, designer; Jo Miller, photo researcher

Photo Credits
The Hubble Heritage Team (AURA/STScI/NASA), 16; iStockphoto/Manfred Konrad, 6; iStockphoto/Soubrette, 4; NASA, 10; NASA/CXC/Rutgers/J. Warren/STScI/U. Ill/Y. Chu/ATCA/U. Ill/J. Dickel, 18; NASA, ESA, and AURA/Caltech, 20; NASA, ESA, and H. Richer (University of British Columbia), 8; NASA, ESA, and the Hubble Heritage Team (STScI/AURA), cover; NASA, ESA, N. Smith (University of California, Berkeley) and The Hubble Heritage Team (STScI/AURA) and NOAO/AURA/NSF, 14; NASA and H. Richer (University of British Columbia), 1; Photodisc, 12